INTERNATIONAL
TRADE
ADMINISTRATION

Manufacturing and Services
Economics Brief

The Impact of Exporting on the
Stability of U.S. Manufacturing Industries

by David Riker and Brandon Thurner

Office of Competition and Economic Analysis

March 2011

Manufacturing and Services Economics Briefs are produced by the Office of Competition and Economic Analysis of the International Trade Administration's Manufacturing and Services unit. A complete list of reports, along with links to other trade data and analysis, is available at *www.trade.gov/mas/ian.*

Acknowledgements

We appreciate the helpful comments that we received from Jeffrey Anspacher, Joseph Flynn, Martin Johnson, Don Lee, Michael Nicholson, and William Powers. All remaining errors are our own.

Table of Contents

Executive Summary

Exporting provides opportunities to expand the sales of U.S. manufacturing industries, resulting in greater revenues for U.S. companies and higher employment for U.S. workers. However, investors and workers are concerned about risk as well as expected return, and risk depends on the volatility of economic outcomes. In the case of exports, it is worth asking whether the added risks and unpredictability associated with exporting outweigh the increase in expected revenues.

In theory, exporting could increase the volatility of the total shipments of U.S. manufacturers by increasing cost competition and by exposing the manufacturers to other types of uncertainty, including exchange rate volatility and fluctuations in shipping costs. On the other hand, exporting could reduce the volatility of their total shipments by diversifying shocks to product demand.

In this paper, we investigate the recent link between exporting and the economic stability of the U.S. manufacturing sector. We compare the volatility of the domestic shipments of U.S. companies and industries to the volatility of their total, worldwide shipments.

First, we analyze the 2000-2009 revenues reported in the public financial statements of two U.S. companies with substantial non-U.S. sales, the Xerox Corporation and the Dow Chemical Company. Both case studies indicate that the companies' non-U.S. revenues reduce the volatility of their total, worldwide revenues.

Second, we analyze industry-level shipments data for the U.S. manufacturing sector from the Annual Survey of Manufactures and the Economic Census for the period 2000-2008. The industry-level data indicate that exporting reduces the volatility of total shipments for a significant majority of the U.S. manufacturing industries. In general, industries with higher export shares experienced larger reductions in the volatility of their total shipments.

1. Introduction

Exporting provides opportunities to expand the sales of U.S. manufacturing industries, resulting in greater revenues for U.S. companies and higher employment for U.S. workers. However, investors and workers are concerned about risk as well as expected return, and risk depends on the volatility of economic outcomes. In the case of exports, it is worth asking whether the added risks and unpredictability associated with exporting outweigh the increase in expected revenues.

In theory, exporting could increase the volatility of the total shipments of U.S. manufacturers by increasing cost competition and by exposing the manufacturers to other types of uncertainty, including exchange rate volatility and fluctuations in shipping costs. On the other hand, exporting could reduce the volatility of the total shipments of U.S. manufacturers by diversifying shocks to product demand. If the second effect dominates, and the volatility of the total shipments of U.S. manufacturers are less than the volatility of their U.S. shipments, then exporting reduces the volatility of the manufacturers' revenue streams. Reducing the volatility of revenues has clear economic benefits. It is valuable to companies and workers that prefer income stability. In addition, reduced volatility can encourage investment in new technologies, physical capital, and human capital.[1]

In this paper, we investigate the recent empirical link between exporting and the economic stability of U.S. manufacturing industries. To measure the volatility of the shipments of U.S. manufacturers, we calculate the ratio of the standard deviation of the unpredictable component of shipments to the most recent value of shipments. We call this ratio the *normalized volatility* of shipments. Since the standard deviation and the most recent value of shipments are measured in the same units, the units cancel from the ratio. This conversion to a percentage, or normalization, facilitates comparison of the volatility measures among companies and industries that vary significantly in size.

We compare the volatility of the domestic shipments of U.S. companies and industries to the volatility of their total, worldwide shipments. First, we examine the 2000-2009 revenues reported in the public financial statements of two U.S. companies with substantial non-U.S.

---

[1] Dixit and Pindyck (1994) provides an excellent introduction to the relationship between investment and uncertainty.

sales, the Xerox Corporation and the Dow Chemical Company.[2] Then we build on these company case studies by analyzing industry-level shipments data for the U.S. manufacturing sector from the Annual Survey of Manufactures (ASM) and the Economic Census for the period 2000-2008.

2. Company Case Study: The Xerox Corporation

The Xerox Corporation (Xerox) is a global document management company that was founded in 1906 and is currently headquartered in Norwalk, Connecticut.[3] The company employs approximately 130,000 people worldwide. It serves non-U.S. markets through a combination of U.S. exports and foreign production, including joint ventures. The company's product offerings include copiers, fax machines, and printers, as well as related services and supplies. The company identifies the reputation of its brands and its innovative technologies as the keys to its international success.

Xerox publicly reports its annual revenues for three geographic areas: the United States, Europe, and Other Areas. It is important to note that the company's non-U.S. revenues are not exclusively exports from the United States. They include sales of goods and services produced by the company's foreign affiliates.[4] The company's exports from the United States are not separately quantified in the company's Annual Reports. This is a limitation on the usefulness of publicly available company data for analyzing the link between exports and the volatility of revenues. (However, this limitation does not apply to the industry-level analysis that we report below.)

Table 1 reports the company's 2000-2009 revenues by geographic area. In 2009, U.S. revenues accounted for 53.7% of the total revenues of Xerox.

---

[2] We analyzed these specific companies because they publicly report their revenues by geographic area, separating U.S. revenues from non-U.S. revenues. This report is not intended to praise or criticize these two companies. It is simply restating information that is published in the companies' public annual reports in terms of our analytical framework.

[3] The following company profile is based on the 2009 Annual Report of the Xerox Corporation.

[4] Likewise, the reported U.S. sales are not necessarily limited to the company's U.S. production. They may include U.S. imports from the company's foreign affiliates.

Table 1: Annual Revenues of the Xerox Corporation by Geographic Segment

Year	U.S. revenues in millions of constant 2008 dollars	Total revenues in millions of constant 2008 dollars	U.S. share of the company's total revenues
2000	13,102	22,947	57.10%
2001	12,008	20,354	59.00%
2002	10,712	18,665	57.39%
2003	9,853	18,100	54.44%
2004	9,356	17,625	53.08%
2005	9,100	17,033	53.43%
2006	8,831	16,699	52.88%
2007	9,272	17,596	52.69%
2008	9,122	17,608	51.81%
2009	8,060	15,000	53.73%

Source: Annual Reports of the Xerox Corporation.

Between 2000 and 2009, the company's annual U.S. revenues ranged from $8.06 billion to $13.10 billion in constant 2008 dollars.[5] Its annual total revenues ranged from $15.00 billion to $22.95 billion over this period. The normalized volatility of the company's total revenues (7.52%) was smaller than the normalized volatility of its U.S. revenues (8.53%), so the company's non-U.S. revenues reduced the normalized volatility of its total revenues.[6]

3. Company Case Study: the Dow Chemical Company

The Dow Chemical Company (Dow) is one of the largest chemical producers in the world.[7] It was founded in 1897 and is headquartered in Midland, Michigan. Dow manufactures and sells chemicals, plastic materials, agricultural products and services, advanced materials and other specialized products and services. The company employs approximately 52,000 people worldwide. The company's success in technological innovation is fueled by annual R&D

---

[5] Throughout this paper, we report all dollar values in 2008 constant dollars.

[6] To measure volatility, we removed the industry-specific mean and linear trend from the shipments data. We discuss this adjustment to the data in the Technical Appendix. The standard deviation is the square root of the average of the squared differences between the variable and its predicted value for each industry and each year. Since there are trends in the data, the predicted values change over time.

[7] This company profile is based on the 2009 Annual Report of the Dow Chemical Company.

expenditures in excess of $1 billion. Dow identifies the geographic balance of its sales as a key to its success.

Dow reports its annual revenues for three geographic areas: the United States, Europe, and the Rest of World. Again, it is important to note that the company's non-U.S. revenues are not exclusively exports from the United States. Table 2 reports the company's 2000-2009 revenues by geographic area.

Table 2: Annual Revenues of the Dow Chemical Company by Geographic Segment

Year	U.S. revenues in millions of constant 2008 dollars	Total revenues in millions of constant 2008 dollars	U.S. share of the company's total revenues
2000	15,971	36,466	43.80%
2001	14,355	33,598	42.72%
2002	13,259	32,514	40.78%
2003	14,771	37,620	39.27%
2004	16,876	45,022	37.48%
2005	19,011	50,235	37.84%
2006	19,092	51,610	36.99%
2007	18,520	54,515	33.97%
2008	18,306	57,361	31.91%
2009	13,978	44,346	31.52%

Source: Annual Reports of the Dow Chemical Company.

In 2009, U.S. revenues accounted for 31.5% of the total revenues of Dow. Between 2000 and 2009, the company's annual U.S. revenues ranged from $13.26 billion to $19.09 billion in constant 2008 dollars. Its annual total revenues ranged from $32.51 billion to $57.36 billion. The normalized volatility of the company's total revenues (11.93%) was smaller than the normalized volatility of its U.S. revenues (14.55%), so the company's non-U.S. revenues reduced the volatility of its total revenues.

4. Analysis of 85 Manufacturing Industries in the U.S. Manufacturing Sector

While the two company case studies provide a measure of the reduction in the normalized volatility of total revenues that results from adding non-U.S. sales to U.S. sales, they do not specifically quantify the contribution of exports from the United States. However, using industry-level data, we can focus the comparisons of normalized volatilities on the shipments of *U.S. production* to the United States and foreign markets. The industry-level analysis also has the advantage that it covers the entire U.S. manufacturing sector, and so it significantly expands the breadth of the analysis.

We analyze publicly available four-digit NAICS industry data on the value of shipments from the ASM for 2000-2001, 2003-2006, and 2008 and from the Economic Census for 2002 and 2007. At this level of disaggregation, there are 85 industries in the U.S. manufacturing sector. The ASM is based on a subset of the population of establishments in the Economic Census. It includes approximately 55,000 manufacturing establishments, with 10,000 large establishments selected with certainty and another 45,000 other establishments selected with probability proportional to establishment size. To be included in the ASM, a manufacturing establishment must have one or more paid employees or leased employees engaged in activities that are classified in NAICS industries 31 through 33.

In order to calculate the domestic shipments of the U.S. industries, we supplement the ASM data with statistics on the free alongside ship value of U.S. domestic exports from the U.S. ITC's Trade Dataweb.[8] We calculate the U.S. shipments of each industry in each year as the difference between its total value of shipments and its domestic exports. Across the 85 industries, the ratio of exports to total shipments in 2008 ranged from 0.6% to 71.7%, with a simple average of 19.1%.

Using these data, we estimate the contribution of exporting to the normalized volatility of the total value of shipments of the U.S. manufacturing industries. Before we report the volatility

---

[8] U.S. domestic exports are produced in the United States. By definition, they include goods from U.S. Foreign Trade Zones that have been enhanced in value. They do not include re-exports. The U.S. International Trade Commission defines the free alongside ship value as "the value of exports at the U.S. port, based on the transaction price, including inland freight, insurance, and other charges. The value excludes the cost of loading the merchandise aboard the carrier and also excludes any further costs."

comparisons for all 85 industries, we will go through a detailed example for a single industry, the Medical Equipment and Supplies Manufacturing industry (NAICS 3391). In 2008, this industry had U.S. shipments of $64.09 billion, and total shipments of $84.03 billion (Table 3).

Table 3: Example of NAICS Industry 3391 (Medical Equipment and Supplies)

Revenues in Billions of 2008 U.S. Dollars

Year	U.S. Shipments Only	Total Shipments	U.S. Share
2000	54.36	66.00	82.36%
2001	56.51	69.13	81.74%
2002	59.86	72.74	82.29%
2003	61.45	75.69	81.19%
2004	59.60	74.86	79.62%
2005	63.77	80.52	79.20%
2006	65.00	82.46	78.83%
2007	61.45	79.81	77.00%
2008	64.04	84.03	76.21%
Ratio of Standard Deviation to 2008 Value	0.029	0.021	

Source: Annual Survey of Manufactures 2000-2001, 2003-2006, 2008; Economic Census 2002, 2007; ITC Trade Dataweb.

The difference between these two numbers is the industry's exports. Between 2000 and 2008, the standard deviation of unpredictable component of the industry's U.S. shipments was $1.78 billion, and the standard deviation of the unpredictable component of its total shipments was $1.84 billion. Although the standard deviation was greater for the U.S. industry's total shipments than for its U.S. shipments, the percentage increase in the standard deviation from expanding the market (3.37%, or 1.84/1.78-1) was smaller than the percentage increase in the 2008 value of shipments (43.12%, or 69.17/48.33-1). It follows that the normalized volatility of the industry's total shipments (2.1%) is less than the normalized volatility of the industry's U.S. shipments (2.9%). We conclude from this comparison that exporting reduced the volatility of the industry's total shipments.[9]

The normalized volatility comparisons for the Medical Equipment and Supplies industry are representative of the results for the 85 manufacturing industries as a whole (The results for each of the industries are reported in a table in the Technical Appendix.). For 21 of the 85 industries, both the normalized volatility and the standard deviation of the industries' total shipments were smaller than their counterparts for the industries' U.S. shipments. The smaller standard deviations for these industries indicate that exports were a particularly good hedge against fluctuations in demand in the U.S. market.[10] For an additional 40 of the 85, the normalized volatility measure was lower for total shipments than for U.S. shipments (but the standard deviation was not), which indicates that exporting reduced the volatility of the shipments of these additional industries relative to their 2008 values.

Among the 85 industries, the Leather & Hide Tanning & Finishing, Audio & Video Equipment, Apparel Accessories & Other Apparel, Communications Equipments and Engine & Turbine & Power Transmission Equipment industries experienced the largest percentage reductions in the normalized volatility of their total shipments as a result of their exports.[11] In general, industries with higher export shares experienced larger reductions in the normalized volatility of their total shipments.

As a sensitivity analysis, we recalculated the normalized volatilities using the mean value of shipments between 2000 and 2008 in the denominator rather than the 2008 value of shipments. The results are similar. For 21 of the 85 industries, both the normalized volatility and the standard deviation of the industries' total shipments were smaller than their counterparts for the industries' U.S. shipments. For an additional 33 of the 85, the normalized volatility measure was lower for total shipments than for U.S. shipments (but the standard deviation was

---

[9] In the Technical Appendix, we identify the technical assumptions that underlie this economic interpretation.

[10] Specifically, they imply that the covariances between the industries' U.S. shipments and their exports were negative.

[11] The NAICS codes for these five industries are 3161, 3343, 3159, 3342 and 3336 respectively.

not), which indicates that exporting reduced the volatility of the shipments of these additional industries relative to their 2008 values.

Finally, we also examined whether the results are different when we focus the analysis on exports to OECD member countries. We defined a U.S. industry's OECD shipments as the sum of its U.S. shipments and its exports to other OECD countries. Of the 85 industries, there are 55 industries for which exports to all countries reduced the normalized volatility of their shipments and exports to other OECD countries also reduced the normalized volatility. There are six industries for which total exports reduced the normalized volatility, but exports to other OECD countries did not. There are two industries for which exports to other OECD countries reduced the normalized volatility of their shipments, but total exports did not.

5. Conclusions

Both the company case studies and the industry-level analysis of the U.S. manufacturing sector indicate that non-U.S. sales, including exports from the United States, reduce the normalized volatility of the value of total shipments of U.S. manufacturers. The value of shipments is a measure of U.S. manufacturers' revenues and not their profits, so the reduction in the volatility of shipments does not necessarily imply a reduction in the volatility of the companies' profits. However, the two are closely connected as long as costs are a steady share of revenues.

References

Bacchetta, Philippe and Eric van Wincoop (2000): "Does Exchange Rate Stability Increase Trade and Welfare?" *American Economic Review* 90(5): 1093-1109.

Bahmani-Oskooee, Mohsen and Scott W. Hegerty (2009): "The Effects of Exchange-Rate Volatility on Commodity Trade between the United States and Mexico." *Southern Economic Journal* 75(4): 1019-1044.

Dixit, Avinash K. and Robert S. Pindyck (1994): *Investment under Uncertainty*. Princeton, N.J.: Princeton University Press.

Ekanayake, E.M., John R. Ledgerwood, and Sabrina D'Souza (2010): "The Real Exchange Rate Volatility and U.S. Exports: An Empirical Investigation." *International Journal of Business and Finance Research* 4(1): 23-35.

Helpman, Elhanan and Paul Krugman (1985): *Market Structure and Foreign Trade*. Cambridge, Massachusetts: MIT Press.

Koray, Faik and William D. Lastrapes (2001): "Real Exchange Rate Volatility and U.S. Bilateral Trade: A VAR Approach." *Review of Economics and Statistics*, 708-712.

Technical Appendix

This appendix provides further details on some of the more technical aspects of the analysis in the paper.

Adjustments to the shipments data to remove predictable trends

In this analysis, we are measuring the unpredictable variation in the shipments series. We are not trying to measure all time series variation in the shipments series, which would include variation in shipments over time due to a deterministic linear trend in the series. For each of the series, we estimated industry-specific means and linear trends for the 2000-2008 sample using Ordinary Least Squares. These simple regression models indicate that there is a positive trend in each series that is statistically significant at the 1% level. On this basis, we conclude that the expected values of the variables are not fixed over time. We calculated the unpredictable component of each of the shipments series as the residuals of its linear trend model.

Next we calculate the standard deviation, which is the square root of the variance. The general definition of variance is that it is the average squared difference between a variable and its expected value. If the expected value happens to be constant over time, then this is the average squared difference between the variable and its time-invariant mean. For these shipments series, however, the expected value is not time-invariant. It increases over time according to the linear trend models. In each year, the actual value of the variable differs from the expected value due to unpredictable variation. When we de-trend the shipment series by subtracting the expected value from the actual value, we are isolating the unpredictable variation, which has mean zero by construction over the 2000-2008 sample period. The de-trending does not require an economic theory about the determinants of the trends or assumptions about whether the trends are the same for U.S. shipments and total shipments or across industries.

We measure the normalized volatility of the shipments data as the ratio of the standard deviation of the residuals to the most recent value of the shipments variable, which is the value in 2008. As a sensitivity analysis, we re-calculate the ratio using the average value for shipments between 2000 and 2008 as the denominator.

Our measure of normalized volatility is similar to the conventional coefficient of variation statistic. However, the coefficient of variation is based on the standard deviation of the original series, not the standard deviation of the unpredictable components of the series. We modify the coefficient of variation statistic to address the predictable trends in the shipment series.

Economic Interpretation of the Comparison of Normalized Volatilities

For industries in which the normalized volatility of total shipments was lower than the normalized volatility of U.S. shipments, we infer that exporting reduces the volatility of the industry's total shipments. This interpretation is based on a counterfactual comparison with specific assumptions. We are assuming that the volatility of the industry's U.S. shipments would be the same in the absence of exports (a hypothetical scenario) as it is with exports (the actual, observed outcome). This is implied by a more technical assumption – that the U.S. industry's marginal cost of production is separable between shipments to the different geographic markets. As long as prices are set based on the U.S. manufacturers' marginal costs, exporting will only affect the value of shipments to the U.S. market if it affects the marginal cost of supplying the U.S. market. If marginal costs are separable between the destination markets, then exporting will not affect the value of shipments to the U.S. market, even if there are fixed costs of production that are shared across the destination markets or fixed costs of accessing export markets.

This technical assumption is consistent with the most common economic models of international trade. It holds if production costs exhibit constant returns to scale, as in the classical Heckscher-Ohlin and Ricardian models of international trade, and the industry is not large enough to have a significant impact on factor prices. It also holds for models with increasing returns to scale and imperfect competition, as long as there are constant marginal costs, as is the case in Helpman and Krugman (1985) and many related models of international trade.

Relation to the Economics Literature

Most of the economics literature that relates volatility to international trade focuses on a single source of uncertainty, exchange rate volatility. Examples of this literature include Bacchetta and van Wincoop (2000), Koray and Lastrapes (2001), Bahmani-Oskooee and Hegerty (2009), and Ekanayake et al. (2010). In contrast, the comparison of normalized volatilities in this paper avoids disentangling the contributions of different sources of uncertainty that are associated with exporting, like fluctuations in aggregate demand in the foreign country, shipping costs, and exchange rates. We demonstrate in this paper that it is not necessary to quantify the separate contribution of each source of volatility in order to determine whether exporting reduced the volatility of an industry's total shipments.

Appendix Table: Ratio of the Standard Deviation to the Value in 2008

NAICS Industry		U.S. Shipments Only	Total Shipments	U.S. Share
3111	Animal food mfg	0.061	0.059	95.34%
3112	Grain & oilseed milling	0.080	0.080	87.55%
3113	Sugar & confectionery product mfg	0.038	0.033	93.23%
3114	Fruit & vegetable preserving & specialty food mfg	0.024	0.025	92.81%
3115	Dairy product mfg	0.040	0.042	96.01%
3116	Animal slaughtering & processing	0.024	0.020	90.34%
3117	Seafood product preparation & packaging	0.043	0.041	95.95%
3118	Bakeries & tortilla mfg	0.015	0.015	97.61%
3119	Other food mfg	0.023	0.020	92.45%
3121	Beverage mfg	0.023	0.020	95.50%
3122	Tobacco mfg	0.114	0.117	97.80%
3131	Fiber, yarn, & thread mills	0.076	0.061	83.05%
3132	Fabric mills	0.129	0.075	63.08%
3133	Textile & fabric finishing & fabric coating mills	0.084	0.069	87.08%
3141	Textile furnishings mills	0.128	0.113	90.39%
3149	Other textile product mills	0.077	0.076	89.99%
3151	Apparel knitting mills	0.209	0.189	87.59%
3152	Cut & sew apparel mfg	0.235	0.234	87.23%
3159	Apparel accessories & other apparel mfg	0.512	0.273	42.59%
3161	Leather & hide tanning & finishing	1.002	0.259	28.30%
3162	Footwear mfg	0.295	0.244	75.53%
3169	Other leather & allied product mfg	0.233	0.201	61.78%
3211	Sawmills & wood preservation	0.137	0.127	90.44%
3212	Veneer, plywood, & engineered wood product mfg	0.177	0.164	92.57%
3219	Other wood product mfg	0.089	0.086	97.02%
3221	Pulp, paper, & paperboard mills	0.039	0.049	84.42%

Appendix Table continued

NAICS Industry		U.S. Shipments Only	Total Shipments	U.S. Share
3222	Converted paper product mfg	0.035	0.032	90.86%
3231	Printing & related support activities	0.042	0.042	93.47%
3241	Petroleum & coal products mfg	0.082	0.084	92.43%
3251	Basic chemical mfg	0.065	0.061	77.11%
3252	Resin, syn rubber, & artificial syn fibers & filaments mfg	0.094	0.075	65.85%
3253	Pesticide, fertilizer, & other agricultural chemical mfg	0.046	0.060	74.12%
3254	Pharmaceutical & medicine mfg	0.034	0.022	78.54%
3255	Paint, coating, & adhesive mfg	0.031	0.030	89.03%
3256	Soap, cleaning compound, & toilet preparation mfg	0.039	0.036	87.86%
3259	Other chemical product & preparation mfg	0.053	0.054	79.92%
3261	Plastics product mfg	0.036	0.035	90.29%
3262	Rubber product mfg	0.041	0.040	79.83%
3271	Clay product & refractory mfg	0.061	0.052	79.55%
3272	Glass & glass product mfg	0.027	0.028	80.49%
3273	Cement & concrete product mfg	0.075	0.075	99.41%
3274	Lime & gypsum product mfg	0.177	0.169	96.19%
3279	Other nonmetallic mineral product mfg	0.045	0.043	88.51%
3311	Iron & steel mills & ferroalloy mfg	0.081	0.079	86.64%
3312	Steel product mfg from purchased steel	0.087	0.086	98.22%
3313	Alumina & aluminum production & processing	0.081	0.084	83.24%
3314	Nonferrous metal (except aluminum) production & processing	0.116	0.115	49.36%

Appendix Table continued

NAICS Industry		U.S. Shipments Only	Total Shipments	U.S. Share
3315	Foundries	0.067	0.068	96.79%
3321	Forging & stamping	0.094	0.093	98.72%
3322	Cutlery & handtool mfg	0.072	0.063	76.93%
3323	Architectural & structural metals mfg	0.063	0.063	97.56%
3324	Boiler, tank, & shipping container mfg	0.045	0.050	90.93%
3325	Hardware mfg	0.044	0.044	77.42%
3326	Spring & wire product mfg	0.033	0.033	88.61%
3327	Machine shops, turned product, & screw, nut, & bolt mfg	0.068	0.068	96.16%
3329	Coating, engraving, heat treating, & allied activities	0.044	0.054	74.79%
3331	Other fabricated metal product mfg	0.057	0.060	53.16%
3332	Agriculture, construction, & mining machinery mfg	0.113	0.144	65.18%
3333	Commercial & service industry machinery mfg	0.069	0.074	65.91%
3334	Ventilation, heating, AC, & commercial refrigeration equip mfg	0.039	0.041	82.78%
3335	Metalworking machinery mfg	0.087	0.088	77.84%
3336	Engine, turbine, & power transmission equipment mfg	0.105	0.040	50.32%
3339	Other general purpose machinery mfg	0.071	0.075	62.42%
3341	Computer & peripheral equipment mfg	0.183	0.177	59.59%
3342	Communications equipment mfg	0.411	0.325	66.78%
3343	Audio & video equipment mfg	0.918	0.224	28.69%
3344	Semiconductor & other electronic component mfg	0.166	0.149	59.02%
3345	Navigational, measuring, medical, & control instruments mfg	0.050	0.050	72.44%
3346	Mfg & reproducing magnetic & optical media	0.053	0.064	92.99%
3351	Electric lighting equipment mfg	0.041	0.043	86.82%

Appendix Table continued

NAICS Industry		U.S. Shipments Only	Total Shipments	U.S. Share
3352	Household appliance mfg	0.060	0.043	79.00%
3353	Electrical equipment mfg	0.093	0.087	69.42%
3359	Other electrical equipment & component mfg	0.149	0.138	71.61%
3361	Motor vehicle mfg	0.160	0.107	72.90%
3362	Motor vehicle body & trailer mfg	0.118	0.111	87.28%
3363	Motor vehicle parts mfg	0.082	0.063	76.40%
3364	Aerospace product & parts mfg	0.096	0.079	49.06%
3365	Railroad rolling stock mfg	0.123	0.114	83.14%
3366	Ship & boat building	0.031	0.020	90.27%
3369	Other transportation equipment mfg	0.082	0.078	88.10%
3371	Household & institutional furniture & kitchen cabinet mfg	0.045	0.040	94.78%
3372	Office furniture (including fixtures) mfg	0.034	0.035	94.43%
3379	Other furniture related product mfg	0.069	0.068	98.14%
3391	Medical equipment & supplies mfg	0.029	0.021	76.21%
3399	Other miscellaneous mfg	0.069	0.031	69.88%

Source: See source note for Table 3.

About the Office of
Competition and Economic Analysis

The Office of Competition and Economic Analysis (OCEA), a part of the International Trade Administration's Manufacturing and Services unit, provides industry and policy decision makers with information on the impacts of economic and regulatory policies on U.S. manufacturing and services industries. Its staff of specialists perform in-depth industry analysis on the effects of both domestic and foreign policy developments on U.S. business competitiveness. For more information, or to access other OCEA reports, visit *www.trade.gov/mas/ian*, or contact the office at (202) 482-5145.

The International Trade Administration's mission is to create prosperity by strengthening the competitiveness of U.S. industry, promoting trade and investment, and ensuring fair trade and compliance with trade laws and agreements.